WHAT'S FAITH GOT TO DO WITH IT? EVERYTHING!

LIVING A LIFE OF FAITH
A Study of Hebrews Eleven

MARK D. PARTIN, D. Min.

RECOMMENDATIONS

This is not your typical presentation of Hebrews 11. Rather than a verse-by-verse exposition or a series of biographical character studies, Mark Partin's new book focuses on the deeper faith principles underlying this great Bible chapter. An insightful and thoroughly biblical writer, Partin shows how the implementation of these important principles are essential to living a practical everyday life of faith. I heartily recommend this beneficial book.

Dr. Danny W. Davis
Senior Pastor, Mount Hermon Baptist Church, Danville, Virginia

In the trying and testing days in which we live with all its uncertainties, Mark Partin's new book, "What's Faith Got To Do With It?", comes as a refreshing oil and an igniter of faith, hope and courage in the heart of the weary, weak and worried. I have read the manuscript and I highly encourage the reading and the re-reading of this timely book.

David Ford, President
Globe for Christ International, Globe, Arizona

Mark Partin's comments on Hebrews Eleven speak to us all, drawing out of his personal victorious Christian life he draws out the rich depths of this marvelous chapter in the New Testament. The results will please the serious student because of its accuracy and insight, and will please the layperson because it is so easy to understand. These pages are clear and fresh they penetrate the heart of the believer to persevere in the battle of living the Christian life. Not much more could be asked of someone that has taken on such a popular chapter in the Bible.

Rev. Phil Taylor
Executive Director of Missions, Bradley County Baptist Association,
Cleveland, Tennessee

AUTHOR'S NOTE

I am deeply indebted to Naomi Craig Johnson for her gracious labor of love in editing and contributing to this text. It is my earnest prayer that as these chapters are read, the Holy Spirit will give each reader a deeper understanding and desire to truly live a life of faith unto the glory of God the Father.

Mark D. Partin

Table of Contents

FORWARD

Since the summer of 2008, anywhere from five to twenty-five prayer intercessors have met on a weekly conference call, crying out to God for revival in Western Christianity.

Each week one of the intercessors, or a pastor or speaker who will be participating at an upcoming Revival Conference, leads out. This means they take ten or fifteen minutes to speak on an aspect relating to the need for revival, around which the team then prays.

On one of those calls Mark Partin was the invited guest. His topic? - The concern that Western Christians might not really be living by faith.

Might it be that in the dulling comforts of Western life, the numbing pressure of Western demands, and, yes – even the passive versions of Western church – we have lost sight of what it means *to live faithfully by faith?*

I was one of the prayer party the night that Mark lead out. A few months later I took on the role of editing and contributing some supporting material to this manuscript — an expression of his heart and mind on the way to recapture a compelling faith.

This meant that for a good period of time, I was immersed in its words and thoughts. They became my close friends. How *very often* they brought comfort, encouragement, and solace to me.

I don't think that was Mark's intention, so much as it is that they incite and awaken to a LIFE that we dare not neglect. But for any who are battle weary and worn from the sometimes arduous seasons of faith — 'eternal vigilance is the price of freedom' — refreshing springs of water await you here, interspersed unsuspectingly among the responsibilities of faith we are summoned to make sure we understand.

I, for one, hope this small book is just the beginning of exploring – no – *of imploring* Western Christians to faithful living.

Because we have everything to lose: our reputations, our comforts, our popularity, our opinions — and much more to gain: the promises, the rewards, and *the reality*.

By FAITH men and women of old gained approval — those of who the world was not worthy. NAOMI CRAIG JOHNSON

INTRODUCTION

If I were to ask you, "What is the most essential element to living a victorious Christian life?"—how would you answer? Is it prayer? Is it worship? Is it Bible study? Is it obeying the Ten Commandments? Is it Christian fellowship? Is it attending church? While all of these are important and I would never discourage any of them, none are the most important element of victorious Christian living. In fact you can participate in all of these religious activities and still live in constant defeat and be in your sin — empty on the inside and not in fellowship with God.

The Pharisees of the New Testament were by far the most religious group of people in their day. They attended the synagogue several times a week, they prayed several times a day, they fasted regularly, and they strived to keep the ceremonial laws and the Ten Commandments. In fact they developed an elaborate set of rules on how a person is to keep the Law. Yet Jesus called them hypocrites, white washed sepulchers, and children of the devil. We must understand that a person can read their Bible and pray faithfully and still be in their sin. You can be kind and giving, helping others, and still be in your sin. How can that be? The Bible teaches us "Whatever is not of faith is sin" (Romans 14:23b). We want to put sin in a box and say it is this or it is that, but God's definition is much simpler — "Whatever is not of faith is sin."

The most essential element for a victorious Christian life is faith. "But without faith it is impossible to please Him" (Hebrews 11:6). "We walk by faith, not by sight" (2 Corinthians 5:7). What we have to understand as Christians then is this — *what does it mean to walk by faith? What does a life of faith look like?*

If you look closely at Hebrews chapter eleven, you see at least ten different aspects of faith revealed.

By faith we gain understanding.

By faith Abel worshipped.

By faith Enoch walked with God.

By faith Noah prepared for the salvation of his family.

By faith Abraham obeyed God.

By faith Sarah's strength was renewed so she could conceive the promised son.

By faith unfulfilled dreams were faced.

By faith parents blessed their children.

By faith Moses made right choices.

By faith adversities were faced.

Over the next several chapters we are going to explore and examine what it means to live a life of faith.

Chapter One

UNDERSTANDING
BY FAITH

By faith we understand that the worlds were
framed by the word of God
Hebrews 11:3

From the beginning God's intention for man has been for man to live by faith. The law was given to show man the futility of trying to live an acceptable life before God on our own, by works. Through out scripture God has called and equipped man to live by faith.

In the Old Testament we are shown what is required of man.

In Deuteronomy 10:12 -13 five conditions are given.

And now, Israel, what does the Lord your God require of you, but to fear the Lord your God, to walk in all His ways and love Him, to serve the Lord your God with all your heart and all your soul, and to keep the commandments of the Lord and His statutes which I command you today for your good?

In Micah 6:8 it is reduced to three conditions.

He has shown you, O man, what is good. And what does the Lord require of you but to do justly, to love mercy, and to walk humbly with your God.

Ecclesiastes 12:13 brings it down to only two conditions.

Fear God and keep His commandments, for this is man's all.

And in Habakkuk 2:4 there is but one condition.

The just shall live by faith.

In the New Testament Paul quotes this Old Testament teaching — "The just shall live by faith" (Romans 1:17*).

God requires man to live by faith. Man is to live by faith so that he can be in relationship with God. God requires man to live by faith, but God also enables man to live by faith. Faith is a gift from God and without the enablement of God man would not be able to live by faith.

So what does it mean to live by faith?

A missionary to the Masai tribe tells of sitting with an elder, talking about the challenges of belief and unbelief. The elder used two languages to respond — his own and Kiswahili. He pointed out that the word the missionaries used to convey faith was not a very satisfactory word in their language. It literally meant 'to agree to'. The missionary knew the word had that shortcoming. The elder said "that 'to believe' like that was similar to a white hunter shooting an animal with his gun from a great distance. Only his eyes and his fingers took part in the act." They should find another word. He said "for a man to really believe it is like a lion going after its prey. His nose and eyes and ears pick up the prey. His legs give him the speed to catch it. All the power of his body is involved in the terrible death leap and single blow to the neck with the front paw, the blow that actually kills. And as the animal goes down the lion envelops it in his arms (Africans refer to the front legs of an animal as its arms) pulls it to himself, and makes it part of himself. This is the way a lion kills. This is the way a man believes."

The missionary looked at the elder in silence and amazement, stunned at the different-tiation. This is what faith is. [1]

It is the overwhelming understanding and conviction of spiritual reality, which then totally governs and shapes the way we live.

Faith is the assurance that God will do what He has said He will do.

It is what gives substance to the promises of God and it is what activates the promises of God.

Faith is walking in the light of God's word and faith is the only response you can have to God and be right with God.

The book of Hebrews, chapter eleven, has been referred to as the Hall of Fame of Faith. It begins by referencing the elders who obtained a good testimony by faith and then moves onto what we understand by faith. Who are the elders? Elders are those who are old and advanced in years. These are individuals who have lived by faith for a long time.

As we move through this chapter several things are shown to us. Truth is revealed. The basis of faith is truth. So we must act on the truth we know. All of these truths must be understood in the context of faith.

In Hebrews 11:1 we are told what faith is, "Now faith is the substance of things hoped for, the evidence of things not seen." This is not so much a definition as it is a statement. In reference to Jesus we read, "Who being the brightness of His glory and the express image of His person, and upholding all things by the word of His power, when He had by Himself purged our sins, sat down at the right hand of the Majesty on high" (Hebrews 1:3). The word for 'person' used here is the same Greek word used for substance in verse 1.[2] It's as if scripture is saying faith is Jesus Christ.

> I have been crucified with Christ: it is no longer I who live, but Christ lives in me; and the life which I now live in the flesh I live by faith in the Son of God, who loved me and gave Himself for me (Galatians 2:20).

Faith always relates to the Person of Jesus Christ.

On several occasions I have been asked about Genesis 1:1 "In the beginning God created the heavens and the earth". I am asked, 'is this fact or fiction'? To be completely honest it is a statement of faith. That is what Hebrews 11:3 expresses when it says, "By faith they understood the world was formed."

Faith gives us understanding. It gives us understanding of God, of creation, and of the Kingdom of God. Faith gives us understanding of purpose, faith gives us understanding of Jesus Christ, and faith gives us understanding of the Holy Spirit. Faith gives understanding.

Why is understanding so important? The Greek word for understand is "noy-eh-o."

It means to comprehend, to examine with the mind, to perceive.[3] The Hebrew word for understanding is "shaw-mad" and it means to hear intelligently, to listen or to obey.[4]

In 1 Kings 3, Solomon was king of Israel. Some commentators suggest he was little more than a teenager at the time. Earlier chapters reveal he had successfully defeated a coup attempt to overthrow his rule by his half brother Adonijah. His father was dead. And now, after he had worshipped and offered sacrifices, we are told God came to him. God told Solomon he could ask for anything and He would give it.

Solomon asked for an understanding heart.

Solomon had faith to know God. Solomon had faith to worship God. He had faith to pray. He had faith to hear God speak. Yet, Solomon asked for an understanding heart.

Hebrews 11:3 tells us that "by faith we understand." In any type of leadership, we need understanding. In ministering to our own families we need understanding. We need understanding in our work place or business. We need understanding in all of life. We need to know that God is near to us and that we are in tune to God. That is the essence of an understanding heart.

In Proverbs 4:23 we are told to "guard our hearts" or to "keep our hearts with all diligence". We must seek God's guidance daily and work so as not to be distracted from a life of faith. The Bible tells us to guard our heart and that "the heart is deceitful above all things" (Jeremiah 17:9). Because of this we must seek an understanding heart.

If we fail to seek an understanding heart we will end up with a divided heart and a deceived heart.

A divided heart is a heart that is not fixed and focused on Christ. It is a heart that has allowed the cares of the world to take priority in one's life. A divided heart is the result of a deceived heart. The heart is deceived when the mind has been defiled. The word defiled means to violate the sanctity of, or to dishonor.[5] When our heart is divided it's because our mind has been overwhelmed and overcome by the world around us. You see this evidenced in a believer's life when they begin to have an up and down walk with God. There is no consistency. They have trouble hearing God speak. And when a believer has trouble hearing God speak, he is in trouble at the heart of his relationship with God. [6]

John's Gospel tells us "My sheep know My voice" (John 10:27). When a believer's mind has been defiled, there is no sense of the presence of God. There is no joy, no boldness, and no sense of awe. A believer's mind or conscience is defiled by harboring sin — by tolerating things in their life known to be wrong. "If I regard iniquity in my heart the Lord will not hear me" (Psalms 66:18). "One who turns away his ear from hearing the law, even his prayer is an abomination" (Proverbs 28:9). "He who covers his sin will not prosper but he who confesses and forsakes them will have mercy" (Proverbs 28:13).

When we refuse to deal with our sin, our sin acts like a hot iron searing the sensitivity of our heart to the point we become numb to the convicting of God's Word and the Holy Spirit. Unforgiveness, bitterness, anger, not having a Christ-like Spirit — all bring about a defiled heart and conscience. "As you did it unto one of the least of these My brethren, you did it to Me" (Matthew 25:40). Have you done or responded to someone lately in a way inappropriate with God's Word? Guard your heart. Just because you can still read the Bible, pray, go to church, and even teach or preach, does not mean your conscience has not been defiled. If you can deliberately violate or neglect God's Word in these areas (unforgiveness, bitterness, anger, or no Christ like spirit), and not be bothered, you are in a dangerous place. The Pharisees went through all the religious motions as well and were highly respected. But they worked against God's kingdom — not for it.

Guard your heart.

Seek an understanding heart.

Be very sensitive to pride and to subtle arrogance slipping in. When you speak ill or disrespectfully to someone and then retell the incident to others, you are bragging about sin. You have already allowed your heart and your conscience to be defiled.

You are far from the presence of God.

Chapter Two

WORSHIPPING
BY FAITH

*By faith Abel offered to God a more excellent sacrifice
than Cain, through which he obtained witness that he was
righteous, God testifying of his gifts; and through
it he being dead still speaks.*
Hebrews 11:4

W orship is the key to experiencing God in our lives. Worship is our response to who God is and what he has done. We were created to worship and glorify God.

But You are holy, enthroned in the praises of Israel (Psalms 22:3*)*.

God has promised to inhabit the praises of His people. It is our worship that provides a meeting place with God. The Amplified Bible reads, "But You are holy, O You who dwell in [the holy place where] the praises of Israel [are offered]."

When it comes to worshipping by faith we are directed to the story of Cain and Abel in Genesis chapter four. After Adam and Eve sinned God did two things for man. First He provided a covering — He slew an animal, shed its blood and covered Adam and Eve with its skin. Then God removed them from the garden. In doing this God showed Adam how He would be approached in worship and I believe God showed Adam where and how He was to be worshipped.

Most of us are familiar with the Holy of Holies in the Tabernacle (see Exodus 37). This was where the mercy seat, covered in blood on the Ark of the Covenant was. On each side of the mercy seat was a golden cherubim (see Exodus 37:9).

After Adam and Eve left the garden, before the flood, I believe the place of worship was at the eastern gate at the Garden of Eden. In the Hebrew text the word "place" in the Hebrew is "sha-kan". It is the word for tabernacle.[7] Here is what scripture says, "God placed (tabernacled) at the east of Eden" (Genesis 3:24). He had the living angels, the cherubim, turning there at 360 degrees. This is where man would come and bring a blood offering. He came to worship God.

So we find there is a right place of worship. In Genesis 4:3 we read "in the process of time." That means that at the end of a number of days, man came to worship. I believe it was the Lord's Day or the Sabbath. We see there was a right time and a right place for worship.

God wants us to understand that He has some expectation of human involvement in worship. We are not to sit back passively and say 'what will be, will be.' There is a certain participation level and passion level that God expects of us in worship. You must be involved — you are to desire it. God desires that we seek Him. Why does God want to be sought? When we put Him first we are saying 'God you are important — so important that you are my priority.' Matthew 6:33 tells us to "seek first the Kingdom of God and His righteousness." If we are going to pursue anyone, it ought to be God. God is the object of our worship. Cain and Abel started out seeking to acknowledge Him as God. But acknowledgement alone is not enough.

Cain and Abel assumed responsibility for passionately, actively, pursuing God. God likes to be passionately pursued. In worship we pursue — we seek God. We approach Him by faith and we reverence Him.

The Hebrew word for worship is "shaha", and it means "to bow down, to prostrate one's self."[8] There are several elements to worship — praise, adoration, prayer, submission, exaltation, and honor. As we present ourselves to God, these are to flow out of our lives by faith.

Cain brought the fruit of the ground, but God requires a blood sacrifice. Cain's offering was not accepted. Abel brought a first fruit from his flock and his offering was accepted.

Herein lies the problem with much of our worship — it is not based in faith. We want to worship God when we want and how we want. This is the spirit of Cain. Cain came to the right place, at the right time, but Cain did not come in faith.

The Bible tells us that "Without the shedding of blood there is no remission" (Hebrews 9:22). Blood is crucial to worshipping in faith. The first time we see blood in the Bible is when God killed an animal to cover Adam and Eve's nakedness because of their sin. There was a substitute and it is here we begin to see substitutionary atonement. The second time blood is spoken of is when Abel brought the blood sacrifice. We see faith being released by obedience to the will and word of God. The third time we see the blood, as a part of worship, is when God told Moses to apply the blood to the door post and the death angel would pass over (see Exodus 12). So when the blood was applied in obedience, and by faith, they were saved.

In Genesis 4 we get down to the basis of worshipping God by faith. This is after the fall of man, and man, in his fallen condition, attempts to worship God. He no longer sits in passivity while God does everything for him. He is to be actively involved and offer sacrifices to God. Whenever you get ready to worship God it is always to be by faith, and faith is demonstrated by our obedience. However, the attitude of the people we worship with affects our ability to worship God. The attitude of worship is crucial. In the New Testament we are told if you are not right with your brother and you find yourself at the place and time of worship, you are to interrupt worship and go and try to make amends with your brother. You are to interrupt the most important thing of your life, worship, and seek reconciliation. Your attitude with other people affects our worship of God.

The Bible tells us that faith comes by hearing and hearing by the word of God. Cain and Abel knew the requirements of God. In spite of knowing the truth, Cain offered what he wanted to offer and expected God to accept it. Whereas Abel worshipped by faith, offering what God asked for. Abel worshipped by faith by pursuing God in obedience as God desires.

"Each of us was created by God for relationship with Him, but we can only enjoy that relationship by God's grace. God's great love for us, demonstrated in Christ Jesus, initiates our response. The only reasonable and adequate response is our expression of worship. And as we worship, God has promised to be present. We can always experience God in worship." [9]

Chapter Three

**WALKING
BY FAITH**

By faith Enoch was taken away so that he did not see death,
'and was not found because God had taken him'; for before
he was taken he had this testimony,
that he pleased God.
Hebrews 11:5

I n Genesis 5: 24 we are told, "And Enoch walked with God, and he was not, for God took him." From this and from the opening Hebrews text we can conclude that a person who walks with God pleases God. Enoch and Noah are the only two people that scripture plainly tells us walked with God. "…Noah was a just man, perfect in his generations. Noah walked with God" (Genesis 6:9). To walk with God means that a person actively chooses to be with God and that he arranges his life around fellowship with God.

Following the statement that Enoch pleased God, we find part of the condition necessary to please or walk with God — "But without faith it is impossible to please Him, for he who comes to God must believe that He is and that He is a rewarder of those who diligently seek Him" (Hebrews 11:6). To walk with God means to believe God and to diligently seek after Him.

There is a tremendous difference between believing God and believing in God. Every Christian will tell you they believe in God. By this they mean they give intellectual assent to the truth of the existence of God. They believe that Jesus was a real person and that He died on the cross. But intellectual assent is not what faith is. Enoch believed in God — he believed in the existence of God. But he went further to the faith aspect. He believed and his belief led him to diligently seek God. God wants us to seek Him. Seek Him first because He is the author and the finisher of our faith. He is the Alpha and Omega, the beginning and the end, the first and the last. He which was, and is, and is to come.

Enoch believed the promise of God.

Now Enoch, the seventh from Adam, prophesied about these men also, saying, 'Behold the Lord comes with ten thousands of His saints, to execute judgment on all, to convict all who are ungodly among them of all their ungodly deeds which they have committed in an ungodly way, and of all the harsh things which ungodly sinners have spoken against Him (Jude 14-15).

What promise? The promise of the savior Jesus Christ. He prophesied of Him. How did Enoch know of the coming Christ? Enoch so walked in fellowship with God, he so walked in agreement and fellowship with Him, that God showed Enoch the Promised One. To walk with God means to actively choose to arrange one's schedule — one's life — around God, in unbroken communion, in unbroken fellowship. It is to have an intimate relationship with God. To have such intimacy, you must pursue God.

This pursuit takes place, I believe, first of all in prayer. Enoch had no Bible to read. Enoch had no church building to go to. What Enoch had was prayer. In prayer Enoch had everything he needed to walk with God.

Enoch walked with God and God rewarded him with insight as to the coming Christ. As a result of his walking with God, Enoch prophesied and witnessed to the truths of God.

How can you and I walk by faith with God?

God has placed eternity in our hearts (Ecclesiastes 3:11).

This means no one has to teach you that *God is* — that He exists.

John 16:8 tells us that the Holy Spirit comes to convict us of sin, of righteousness, and of judgment.

> But without faith it is impossible to please Him, for he who comes to God must believe that He is and that He is a rewarder of those who diligently seek Him (Hebrews 11:6).

We begin by recognizing God — the God of the Bible, the only true and living God. Once God has our attention we follow Him. We follow the leading of the Holy Spirit. The Holy Spirit shows us our lostness. The Holy Spirit enables us to be saved by faith. The Holy Spirit is the one that prompts us to call out to God unto salvation. The Holy Spirit seals us and the Holy Spirit is there to fill us fresh daily so we can be sensitive to God's leading. We become attentive to God. We learn to listen to God.

Listening to God is part of prayer. In Luke eighteen we are told that two men went up to the temple to pray. Only one left justified. Why? Dr. Francois Carr of Heart Cry, South Africa says, "Prayer is not so much about being in the place of prayer, as it is being prepared to hear God." Before we pray, we must have an expectancy that we will hear God speak to us. We must be prepared to enter his presence. 1 Kings 3 tells us the story of King Solomon's prayer. After he had worshipped and was alone, God came to Solomon. Why? Solomon loved God (see I Kings 3:3). Do you love God?

Love implies a relationship. A relationship is about intimacy. When you have a relationship there will be several things evidenced in your life. There is a partnership that will involve sharing, communication and accountability. All of these things are involved in a love relationship. A love relationship is what God seeks from us. God came to Solomon because Solomon loved God. God wants to come to us and to speak to us. Are you in a position to hear God? Are you attentive to God's voice?

God speaks in a still small voice to our hearts. He speaks to us through the Bible, the Word of God. He will never tell us anything in contradiction to the truth of the Bible. God speaks to us through the Holy Spirit who has taken up residence in your life. The Holy Spirit wants to be more than resident in your life — he wants to be president of your life. This takes place as we walk by faith. In walking by faith we abandon our own wants and wishes. Jesus said, "My food is to do the will of Him who sent me and to finish His work" (John 4:34). "If anyone desires to come after Me, let him deny himself, and take up his cross and follow Me" (Matthew 16:24*)*. As we abandon our self and our wants and we allow the Holy Spirit to fill us fresh daily, we become more and more sensitive to His prompting in our lives.

God's speaking to us is a great reward. One of the main teachings in EXPERIENCING GOD about being on mission with God and following Christ is that we must make major adjustments in our lives to God. After you make adjustments from walking by sight, to walking by faith, you then daily adjust your life to God.[10] It is an act of fine tuning your life.

This is another aspect of walking with God by faith. Our goal should not be to formulate plans and ask God to bless them but to get on God's plan and watch Him work on us and through us.

> No longer do I call you servants, for a servant does not know what his master is doing; but I have called you friends, for all things that I heard from My Father I have made known to you (John 15:15).

A lot of Christians lose the victory because their lives are spent trying to serve the Lord, rather than diligently seeking the Lord.

Mary sat at the feet of Jesus and listened to Christ. Martha was distracted with many things (see Luke 10:39-42). When you are obeying Him as the Holy Spirit leads and guides you, and you are depending on Him, God will work in your life and through your life. The activity of God begins to be demonstrated in you. It was when Moses, led by God, went back to Egypt, that he then began to see God working in him and through him.

The Bible has a lot to say about how a believer walks with God by faith.

We are to walk in love.

> Therefore be imitators of God as dear children. And walk in love as Christ also loved us and given Himself for us… (Ephesians 5:1-2).

We are to walk in Christ.

> As you therefore have received Christ Jesus the Lord, so walk in Him (Colossians 2:6).

We are to walk in light.

> But if you walk in the light as He is in the light, we have fellowship with one another, and the blood of Jesus Christ His Son cleanses us from all sin (1 John 1:7.)

We are to walk in truth.

> I rejoiced greatly that I have found some of your children walking in truth, as we received commandment from the Father (2 John 4). For Your lovingkindness is before my eyes, and I have walked in your truth (Psalm 26:3).

We are to walk in newness of life.

> Therefore we were buried with Him through baptism into death, that just as Christ was raised from the dead by the glory of the Father, even so we also should walk in newness of life (Romans 6:4).

We are to walk in the Spirit.

> I say then: Walk in the Spirit, and you shall not fulfill the lust of the flesh (Galatians 5:16).

We are to walk worthy of our calling and vocation.

> I, therefore, the prisoner of the Lord, beseech you to walk worthy of the calling with which you were called (Ephesians 4:1).

We are to walk carefully.

> See then that you walk circumspectly, not as fools but as wise (Ephesians 5:15).

We are to walk as Christ walked.

> He who says he abides in Him ought himself also to walk just as He walked (1 John 2:6).

We are to walk worthy — in purity and holiness.

> You have a few names even in Sardis who have not defiled their garments, and they shall walk with Me in white, for they are worthy (Revelation 3:4).

When Elisabeth Elliot lived in the Ecuadorian forest in the 1950's, she usually traveled on foot and always had a guide with her. Only once did she go off alone and "quickly learned what a bad mistake that was." The guide either knew the way or knew much better than she did how to find it. The trails often led through streams and rivers across which she "had to wade, but sometimes there was a log laid high above the water which we had to cross."

"I dreaded those logs and was always tempted to take the steep, hard way down into the ravine and up the other side. But the Indians would say, 'Just walk across, senorita,' and over they would go, confident and light footed."

Elisabeth was barefoot as they were, but it was not enough. On the log, she couldn't keep from looking down at the river below. She knew she would slip. "I had never been any good at balancing myself on the tops of walls and things, and the log looked impossible." So her guide would stretch out a hand, and the touch of it was all she needed. She stopped worrying about slipping. She stopped looking down at the river or even at the log and looked at the guide, who held her hand with only the lightest touch.

"The lesson the Indians taught me," Elisabeth says, "was that of trust. If I had been inclined to come to a halt in the middle of the log and raise nasty questions or argue their ability to keep me from falling, my trust would have collapsed and so would I." [11]

To walk worthy is the greatest challenge, but it is not dependent on our righteousness or strength, but the righteousness and strength of Jesus Christ as it is imputed to us *by faith*.

The King James rendering of our opening text reads "By faith Enoch was taken away so that he should not see death; and was not found, because God had taken him: for before he was taken he had this testimony, that he pleased God" (Hebrews 11:5). Strong's Concordance defines the word taken or translate as "to transfer or to exchange." [12] I see simply that when we walk with God by faith we also will be changed. The old will pass away and the new will come. "To be conformed to the image of His Son…" (Romans 8:29). The term 'translated' is the Biblical theology of being changed by God. The same word translated was used for Christ on the Mount of Transfiguration (see Luke 9:28-31). In Luke's Gospel we are told that as Jesus prayed, He was transfigured. As he spent time with

Moses who represents the Law, and Elijah who represented the prophets, Jesus was transfigured — changed. Being changed by God is connected to prayer and abiding in the word of God.

> I beseech you therefore, brethren, by the mercies of God, that you present your bodies a living sacrifice, holy, acceptable to God, which is your reasonable service. And do not be conformed to this world but be ye transformed by the renewing of your mind, that you may prove what is that good and acceptable and perfect will of God (Romans 12:1-2).

In the Greek the word for 'transformed' used here is the same word 'translated' used of Enoch. It means to be changed.

In 2 Corinthians 3, we read the story of Moses wearing a veil on his face because of the glory of his countenance — he had spent time in the presence of God. In verse eighteen we read, "But we all, with unveiled face, beholding as in a mirror the glory of the Lord, are being transformed into the same image from glory to glory, just as by the Spirit of the Lord." Paul used the example of a mirror because during New Testament time mirrors were not made of glass but of polished metals.[13] As these were polished and continually refined reflections became clearer. These mirrors were nothing compared with modern day mirrors of glass but Paul used this illustration because just as the mirror was in the process (present imperative mood—*continually being changed*) so we too are in the process of beholding the glory of God and are also being continually changed. We are changed from one degree of glory into another as by the Spirit of the Lord. The mirror we look in today is the Word of God.

God is able to change us. Have you been changed lately? Are you closer to God today than you were last year?

When the writer of Hebrews says Enoch was translated or changed, this is a basic understanding of the life transformed by

God. It refers to the believer's progressive sanctification. It comes by prayer, by spending time in the presence of God, by abiding in the Word of God, and by the Word of God abiding in you.

Do you know anything about the transformation process of God? Traditions and mere ceremonial religion have no power to sanctify and change. We must gaze upon Christ — we must fix the focus of our lives upon Christ. A passing glance will not suffice. An hour on a Sunday will not be enough. We must fix our eyes upon the living Lord. The transformation is slow but it is sure.

The Holy Spirit will not cease to work in us to transform us into the image of Christ. But it will not come to completion until we behold Him — until we see the risen and the living Lord.

Chapter Four

**PREPARING FOR THE SALVATION
OF YOUR FAMILY
BY FAITH**

By faith, Noah, being divinely warned of things not yet
seen, moved with godly fear, prepared an ark for the saving
of his household, by which he condemned the world and
became heir of the righteousness which is
according to faith.
Hebrews 11:7

How do you respond to warnings? Tobacco products come with a warning from the surgeon general, "This product may be dangerous to your health." Roadways come with warnings: curves ahead, slow down, falling rock zone, use caution.

On April 26, 1986 one of the worst nuclear accidents in history occurred at the Chernobyl reactor in the Ukraine. The cause of the Chernobyl disaster was readily identified — gross negligence on the part of plant operators. Thirty people died and many more suffered illness as a result of radiation exposure. Several safety and cooling systems had been disengaged and other unauthorized actions had occurred during tests of electrical equipment.[14] Gross negligence and failure to heed warning signs cost many people their lives. Failure to heed warnings can cost people eternity apart from Christ.

Noah was divinely warned by God of the coming judgment He was going to bring to mankind. According to Genesis six, we are told that Noah walked with God. When a person walks with God, as we have said earlier, that person is in a position to hear God. Because of Noah's life and life style, he heard the warning.

But Noah found grace in the eyes of the Lord. This is the genealogy of Noah. Noah was a just man, perfect in his generation. Noah walked with God. And Noah begot three sons: Shem Ham, and Japheth. The earth also was corrupt before God, and the earth was filled with violence (Genesis 6:8-11).

The condition of planet earth has regressed back to the condition of Noah's day. In fact it appears to be even worse.

> But as the days of Noah were, so also will the coming of the Son of Man be. For as in the days before the flood, they were eating and drinking, marrying and giving in marriage, until the day that Noah entered the ark. And did not know until the flood came, and took them all away, so also will the coming of the Son of Man be (Matthew 24: 37-39).

People of our day are very much like the people of Noah's day. They are so caught up in life — eating and drinking, buying and selling. They are so caught up in family that they fail to hear the warning of God. Life goes on as usual, but one day Jesus Christ will return. You must be prepared for His return and you must be preparing your family for His return. One of the saddest things I see happening in the American Church today is that instead of preparing and teaching our families to be a part of the people of God and to be a part of the church, many are teaching their families to depart from the church — the body of Christ, the Bride of Christ. We act as if we have all the time in the world to get ready for the coming of Christ. Peter cut off the ear of Malchus, because he was not listening to Jesus, and in doing so Malchus could not hear. Often the lives we live as believers prevent others from hearing the warnings of scripture.

How do we teach our families and our children to depart from church? We use Sunday as a family day. We make plans on Sunday to do things and visit people so we don't have time for church. We schedule events, activities, go to sport competitions and act as if it is perfectly alright with God to misuse the Lord's Day. We justify ourselves the entire time. Then we see the outcome as our college age children leave home — they also leave the church.

Why?

'If the church, the Body of Christ, is not important for my parents, it is certainly not important for me.' Now this is not true in every case, but for many it is. It is amazing what we let come before the Lord on Sunday. And then we never think of our need to repent over our sin of forsaking the church or of violating one of the Ten Commandments.

How do we find grace in the eyes of God, as Noah did? In all honesty grace finds us and we have to choose to respond to it. Our only response is faith.

For by grace you have been saved through faith, and that not of yourselves; it is the gift of God (Ephesians 2:8).

The gift of God, the ultimate gift of God, is grace freely given to all who will receive it by faith.

Noah lived in a difficult time. Noah lived in a time when it was not popular to serve God. Violence and wickedness prevailed, peer pressure was everywhere. Noah lived in a time when other things could take precedence over God. But Noah was a just man. That means Noah's conduct was free of any wrong. Noah was perfect — he was blameless — he was completely obedient to God and His word. Noah walked with God. Noah actively chose to be with God. He arranged his life around that fellowship. How did Noah do this? He found grace in the eyes of God (see Genesis 6:8).

The only way we can prepare our families for salvation is because of the grace of God. Grace comes first. As we adjust our lives to God, we make preparation for our families.

Do you heed the warnings that God still gives today? All through scripture Christians are given a series of caution lights. We are warned of the dangers that come into the life of a Christian when he thinks he can play with sin or live outside the Body of Christ.

Therefore let him who thinks he stands, take heed lest he fall (I Corinthians 10:12).

Some Christians feel immune to temptation. They live as if 'it will never happen to me.' I can come and go as I please, do whatever I want, when I want, and nothing will happen to me or my family. Again, one of the saddest things I see is Christian moms and dads taking their unsaved children away from church, going on family outings or to recreation parks and events on Sunday, while not realizing that instead of preparing their family for salvation, they are instead preparing for their turning away from God.

The Bible clearly shows that the child of God never gets to the point where he cannot be tempted by sin, or where he is beyond the ability of the devil to cause problems. We have played with sin, laughed at sin, and minimized sin. But the Bible says, "At the last it bites like a serpent and stings like a viper" (Proverbs 23:32).

No temptation has overtaken you except such as is common to man; but God is faithful, who will not allow you to be tempted beyond what you are able, but with the temptation will also make the way of escape, that you may be able to bear it (I Corinthians 10:13).

God gives us warnings and as we seek him diligently, we see the escape route He provides. We are responsible to act on what He says. God is faithful to provide but we must abide in Him.

Noah was divinely warned — he heeded God's warning of coming judgment. It is worth noting that the warning came and that it was one hundred and twenty years later that the judgment fell. We have been warned — don't put off what you know is right. Don't play with your family's spiritual health.

Noah was "moved with godly fear." What does it mean to fear God? The fear of God is part of you and me preparing for the salvation of our families. There are between one- hundred-and-fifty and one-hundred-and-seventy references in the Word of God about the fear of the Lord.

The fear of God, or the fear of the Lord, is defined as dread or terror of God for an unsaved person. For the Christian it means to honor, to reverence, to venerate God.

Once a person is saved God places His fear in that person's life (see Jeremiah 32:40).

These are the essential ingredients of the fear of God:

- Correct concepts of the character of God. We recognize His holiness, His majesty, His immensity.
- A pervasive sense of God's presence. God's presence has a controlling effect on us. We are constrained, as Paul says, by the love of God.
- A constant awareness of our obligation to God. We are to love Him supremely. We are to obey Him implicitly. We are to trust Him completely.[15]

When a person lacks the fear of God it is seen in an over attachment to the things of the world, such as materialism, sports, and travel. And it is seen in an under attachment to the things of God — things that are heavenly or spiritual.

Noah feared God, and he prepared for the salvation of his family. "Noah perfected the act of obedience — not the art of thinking about obedience."[16]

How did he prepare? He built an ark, a place of safety. For about one hundred years he built that place of safety. Even when he and his family were mocked and ridiculed, he still built that ark. In our day, even amidst ridicule and mockery, we must be building the place of safety for our families. We can't afford to be distracted by the cares and things of this world. We can't be dissuaded by peer pressure. We must build for our families a place of safety and security.

Everyday that Noah got up and worked on the ark, he was giving testimony to his family that he was seeking God. Everyday that he got up and worked, with each nail he hammered, he was bearing testimony of the coming judgment of God. Everyday Noah ignored the ridicule of man, he was bearing testimony to God "...and became heir of the righteousness which is according to faith" (Hebrews 11:7).

How do we prepare for the salvation of our family? Heed the warnings of God. Even when there is no sign of rain, prepare for the storm. Fear God — let it control you. Build in accordance with God's Word. Exercise faith in such a way that you are known not merely as a good, moral, family man but as a man who seeks after God. Whatever you do for a living, use it as a platform to share the message of Christ. Through your work glorify God. Just as Noah entered the ark and was safe, he still faced the storm. Today I believe the church is our spiritual ark that we find security in to face the storms and challenges of life. The church is the vehicle God has ordained to carry us through the difficulties of life.

We desperately need the church.

Chapter Five

OBEYING GOD
BY FAITH

By faith Abraham obeyed when he was called to go out to
the place which he would receive as an inheritance. And
he went out not knowing where he was going.
Hebrews 11:8

Tr鈥攔ue faith is a gift from God. God enables those who come to Him to respond and to receive the ability to exercise true saving faith — biblical faith. Read and listen to the following scripture verses carefully.

For by grace you have been saved through faith, and that not of yourselves; it is the gift of God (Ephesians 2:8).

For in it the righteousness of God is revealed from faith to faith; as it is written, 'The just shall live by faith' (Romans 1:17).

Therefore having been justified by faith, we have peace with God through our Lord Jesus Christ (Romans 5:1).

So Jesus said to them, 'Because of your unbelief; for assuredly I say to you, if you have faith as a mustard seed, you will say to this mountain, 'Move from here to there,' and it will move and nothing will be impossible for you' (Matthew 17:20).

But the fruit of the Spirit is love, joy, peace, longsuffering, kindness, goodness, faithfulness (Galatians 5:22).

For we walk by faith, not by sight (2 Corinthians 5:7).

For whatever is not from faith is sin (Romans 14:23b.)

But without faith it is impossible to please Him (Hebrews 11:6a).

Do you believe God meant what he said in these verses?

How are you saved? How are you justified? How are you at peace with God? How are you to approach God? How are you to move mountains and accomplish the impossible? How are you to please God? How are you to live?

The answer keeps going back to the same thing — *by faith.*

Abraham obeyed God by faith. It is not possible to live by faith without having obedience flowing from our lives and characterizing our lives. However, it is possible to obey the Word of God and still not be living by faith. That is where many people are today. Our churches are filled with people who obey in action but they do not live by faith.

We often say about people who are always at church — 'they are so faithful.' Being faithful in attendance to church worship and church activities is commendable but it is not faith. Faith involves our whole life. Faith involves living by the Spirit and not by our flesh. The place we are to start is in being led by the Spirit. "The problem is many believers want to start with obedience. We know what God expects of us and we constantly struggle to do what is right and avoid what is wrong. When we try to be obedient in our own effort it leads to futility. Obedience must begin with the foundation of faith, believing and accepting the truth and promises of the Word of God. Many find the victory elusive and efforts to live an obedient Christian life a failure because they have not built their efforts on a foundation of faith, renewal of the mind, and commitment to be led by the Spirit." [17]

It is very easy to truly come to saving faith in Christ and then to attempt to live for Christ in our own strength. We often mimic what we see other believers doing. "Many Christians have what we might call a 'cultural holiness'. They adapt to the character and behavior pattern of Christians around them. As the Christian culture around them is more or less holy, so these Christians are more or less holy. But God has not called us to be like those around us. He has called us to be like Himself. The level of our obedience is most often determined by the behavior standard of other Christians around us." [18] We go through the motions and we are moral but we never come to the place where we truly live by faith and obey by faith. Faith is foundational to our obedience.

In Galatians three we are warned about coming to Christ and receiving the Holy Spirit and then reverting back to the law and works. Obedience to God begins by a work of the Holy Spirit with conviction, and as we respond to the Holy Spirit the Spirit continues to teach us and guide us.

> And do not be conformed to this world, but be transformed by the renewing of your mind, that you may prove what is that good and acceptable and perfect will of God (Romans 12:2).

Abraham obeyed God by faith. The way we obey God by faith is by constantly renewing our mind in Him. If we fail to renew our minds we will conform to the world around. The world will squeeze us into its mold. To renew your mind is to allow the Bible and the Holy Spirit to change the way you think. We begin to think Biblically and spiritually. When the way we think conforms to scripture, then the way we see the world around us will change. We will see though the eyes of God.

How did Abraham renew his mind? If you study the life of Abraham you recognize that he was not perfect in all his doings. He sinned, he made bad decisions, and he had struggles — just as we do. But the one thing about Abraham you find consistently throughout his life is that Abraham was always building altars to God. An altar represents a meeting with God — a time of worship, reflection, and guidance.

There are five altars recorded in scripture that Abraham built.

- Abram passed through the land to the land of Shechem, as far as the terebinth tree of Moreh. And the Canaanites were then in the land. Then the Lord appeared to Abram and said, 'To your descendants I will give this land.' And there he built and altar to the Lord, who appeared to him (Genesis 12:6-7).
- And he moved there to the mountain east of Bethel, and he pitched his tent with Bethel on the west and Ai on the east; there he built an altar to the Lord and called on the name of the Lord (Genesis 12:8).
- And he went on his journey from the South as far as Bethel, to the place where his tent had been at the beginning, between Bethel and Ai, to the place of the altar which he had made first. And there Abram called on the name of the Lord (Genesis 13:3-4).
- Then Abram moved his tent, and went and dwelt by the terebinth trees in Mamre, which are in Hebron, and built an altar there to the Lord (Genesis 13:18).
- Then they came to the place of which God had told him. And Abraham built an altar there, and placed the wood in order; and he bound Isaac his son and laid him on the altar, upon the wood (Genesis 22:9).

Robert Murray McCheyne has said, "It is the look that saves, but it is the gaze that sanctifies."[19] Abraham not only looked to God for salvation (see Romans 4:16-25) but Abraham gazed at the Father, as seen by the altars he built for his sanctification. Sanctification is the process of having our minds renewed. Abraham lived his life before the altar of God. His worshipping at the altar points to the path of understanding how we today are to advance in our walk of faith and obedience. From the opening pages of Genesis we see Abraham's altar experiences unfolding like a chain reaction of growth in faith, revealing a worshipping believer who moves forward in his walk with God.

The first altar in Genesis 12:7, near Shechem, shows that the first point of faith is to be open and receptive to God's promises even when it seems that they are beyond our ability to contain. Receive the promise — the truth of God. God promised Abraham an enormous amount of land. We do not know the thoughts that went through his mind but he was probably shocked by God's word. The Bible says, "He did not waver at the promise of God…" (Romans 4:20). It does not say he was not surprised. When God gives you a promise you must personally claim it. You must make sure your life is in line with the conditions surrounding the promise.

What is meant by this word — conditions? If I were to tell you, 'If you mow my lawn, I will pay you fifty dollars,' the condition of payment is on you mowing my lawn. The promises of the Bible are always with conditions. "For whoever calls on the name of the Lord shall be saved" (Romans 10:13). The condition is on your calling on God. "And my God shall supply all your need according to His riches in glory by Christ Jesus" (Philippians 4:19). The condition of this verse in its context is in first giving an obedient offering to the Lord. When the condition is met, then you have the right to claim the promise.

With the second altar near Bethel in Genesis 12:8 this statement is made, "and (Abram) called on the name of the Lord." This points to a growing knowledge of God. The 'name' of the Lord reflects His nature, His person, His character. As Abram journeyed onward and faced the tough issues of life, he was claiming the trustworthiness of God — and so can we. As we walk by faith and obey God by faith, we grow in our knowledge of the trustworthiness of God.

The names of God are an amazing study. In the names of God, God's unique character traits are discovered.

- Jehovah — the self existing one who reveals Himself
  Sing to God, sing praises to His name. Extol Him who rides on the clouds, By His name Yah, and rejoice before Him (Psalm 68:4).
- Jehovah-M'Kaddesh — the Lord who sanctifies
  Speak also to the children of Israel, saying, 'Surely My Sabbaths you shall keep, for it is a sign between Me and you throughout your generations, that you may know that I am the Lord who sanctifies you (Exodus 31:13).
- Jehovah-Nissi — the Lord our victory
  And Moses built an altar and called its name, 'The–Lord-Is-My–Banner (Exodus 17:15).
- Jehovah-Jireh — the Lord our provider
  And Abraham called the name of the place, The-Lord-Will-Provide; as it is said this day, 'In the Mount of the Lord it shall be provided (Genesis 22:14).
- Jehovah-Tsidkenu — the Lord our righteousness
  In those days Judah will be saved, and Jerusalem will dwell safely. And this is the name by which she shall be called: The Lord Our Righteousness (Jeremiah 33:16).
- Jehovah-Rohi — the Lord our shepherd
  The Lord is my Shepherd; I shall not want (Psalm 23:1).
- Jehovah-Shammah — the Lord is present
  All the way around shall be eighteen thousand cubits; and the name of the city from that day shall be: THE LORD IS THERE (Ezekiel 48:35).

The third altar in Genesis 13:4 is the same place as the second altar. Along the way of life Abram made a detour to Egypt. This trip was not directed by God and was characterized by compromise on Abram's part. There was a famine and Abram went to Egypt seeking food. His method was the pursuit of personal supply in the wisdom of his own way. Abram drifted from God. I have certainly done this in my own life on occasion. The purpose of this altar is simple — the point of departure is the point of return or restoration. There Abram found abundant pardon from God. In 2 Kings 6 the story is told of the prophets cutting down trees in order to enlarge their territory. One man lost his axe head in the river. When Elisha came on the scene they returned to the place the axe head was lost and found it floating on the water. Yes, a miracle took place but the main thrust is 'the point of departure is the point of return and restoration.'

The fourth altar, mentioned in Genesis 13:14-18 was near Hebron. Reestablished in the land, Abram was challenged again by God. Earlier God had said land would be given. Now God specifies divisions — northward, southward, eastward and westward. "Arise, walk in the land through its length and its width, for I give it to you" (Genesis 13:17). God had said, "I will give this land" (Genesis 12:7). Now God says, "I give it to you." Here we find the fulfillment of the promise. Abraham's borders have been enlarged. His horizon of hope has increased.

It is at the fifth and final altar, in Genesis twenty-two, where Abraham is called to offer his promised son as a sacrifice to God. Jesus said, "Your father Abraham rejoiced to see My day, and he saw it and was glad" (John 8:56). Abraham saw Jesus in the Old Testament and I believe Jesus was referencing this very incident because Abraham got a first hand lesson about Christ, Calvary and the cross. Here you see a clear picture of what the Bible is all about — the Savior dying for the sins of the world.

Abraham had waited one hundred years for his son, Isaac. He was a son of promise and prophecy, just like Jesus. All Abraham's hopes and dreams were wrapped up in that young man and God now asked Abraham to give up his son of promise forever, to offer him as a sacrifice upon the altar. This is ultimate sacrifice — to give your most precious possession. Can you imagine how that must have drained the very life out of Abraham? His heart sank, his knees buckled, his stomach twisted in knots. For a brief moment despair, doubt, and disillusionment flooded his soul.

Elisabeth Elliot has said, "Either we are adrift in chaos or we are individuals created, loved, upheld, and placed purposefully, exactly where we are. Can you believe that? Can you trust God for that?" [20] Every experience or trial puts you to the test: Do you trust God or don't you? [21]

This fifth altar Abraham built was the last one recorded. It was an altar that came late in his life. It came after years of obedience and faith and it was the altar of ultimate surrender. No one will ever think they are prepared to build this altar or to face this altar. But God knows.

As Abraham and Isaac went to the mountain of sacrifice, Isaac carried the wood. Just as Isaac had to bear that wood up that mountain, Jesus had to bear His cross up His mountain.

Three times we are told that Abraham and Isaac went to the 'place' which God had told them. Where was this place? — Mt. Moriah (see Genesis 22:2). It was neither coincidence nor accident. Moriah means "foreseen by God, vision, the shown of Jehovah."[22]

In the mind of God there was no other place like this place. Eventually the temple would be built on Mt Moriah (see 2 Chronicles 3:1). And much later, Jesus Christ would die for us on this same mount (see Luke 23:33). Before the sun began to shine and the stars were hung in space — before the planets were spun into orbit, before the foundation of the world — the Lamb of God was slain on that place called Moriah which means foreseen by God.

Abraham obeyed God and offered his son. At just the right time God called to Abraham and stayed his hand from the sacrifice. God then provided a ram that had been caught in the thicket. So a lamb died instead.

Abraham called the place "Jehovah Jireh" meaning "the Lord shall provide." All through out Abraham's life God had provided, but on this day Abraham came in complete surrender and he recognized Jehovah Jireh. He recognized the trustworthiness of God through surrender.

Abraham obeyed God by faith because the foundation of his life was faith. His mind was regularly renewed as he built altar after altar to God.

When was the last time you had your mind renewed? Where was the last altar you built — the last significant place you met with God?

Chapter Six

THE PROMISE CONCEIVED
BY FAITH

By faith Sarah herself also received strength to conceive
seed, and she bore a child when she was past the age,
because she judged Him faithful who had promised.
Hebrews 11: 11

S arah received strength to conceive seed. Think about that for
a moment, faith to conceive seed. God will give you strength
for conception to take place if you act in faith to God. I am not
talking about becoming pregnant with a new baby. I am talking
about becoming pregnant with truth. Allowing the seed, the Word of
God, to be planted in us, and us allowing the truth of God to bring
forth fruit in our lives.

Jesus told the parable of the sower in Matthew thirteen.

Then He spoke many things to them in parables, saying:
'Behold a sower went out to sow. And as he sowed some seed
fell by the wayside; and the birds came and devoured them.
Some fell on stony places, where they did not have much
earth; and they immediately sprang up because they had no
depth of earth. But when the sun was up they were scorched
and because they had no root they withered away. And some
fell among thorns and the thorns sprang up and choked them.
But others fell on good ground and yielded a crop: some a
hundred fold, some sixty, some thirty' (Matthew 13:3-8).

Then He explained the parable.

Therefore hear the parable of the sower: 'When anyone
hears the word of the kingdom, and does not understand it,
then the wicked one comes and snatches away what was
sown in his heart. This is he who received seed by the wayside. But he who receives the seed on stony places, this is he

who receives the word and immediately receives it with joy; yet he has no root in himself, but endures only for a while. For when tribulation or persecution arises because of the word, immediately he stumbles. Now he who received seed among thorns is he who hears the word, and the cares of this world and the deceitfulness of riches choke the word, and he becomes unfruitful. But he who received seed on good ground is he who hears the word and understands it, who indeed bears fruit and produces; some a hundredfold, some sixty, some thirty' (Mathew 13:18-23).

We started this book talking about *understanding by faith*. Here once again we see the importance of an understanding heart. To receive the Word of God takes an understanding heart. There are four types of soil mentioned in this parable. Each person has each soil in their lives, so we are all in the same condition.

The seed is the word of God. When God's word is broadcast by the sower, be it through proclamation, teaching, or reading, if it is not acted on the devil will steal it away so that there is no possibility of the truth coming to conception in your heart. When truth does not conceive in your heart, it is as if you have a miscarriage. The truth of God never comes to fruition in your life.

So how are you to receive the Word of God? By listening for God to speak and when God speaks you must process the truth that you hear. "For me, it is wonderfully reassuring to know that this does not mean knowing all the word, being perfectly obedient to all the word, at one time. Hearing one thing, doing that one thing, is what is required."[23] The issue comes back to our processing truth. When you encounter truth, you have encountered God. Then you have to process it. This means you have to absorb it and let it flow to every area of your life. You adjust your life to the truth.

In Mark six we are told the story of Jesus feeding five thousand men with five loaves and two fish. There were twelve baskets of leftovers when everyone had eaten. The disciples got into a boat and headed across the sea while Jesus went to the mountain to pray. The wind blew against them as the disciples struggled to get across the sea. Then Jesus came to them, walking on the water, and the disciples were troubled thinking he was a ghost. Jesus immediately spoke words of comfort to them, got into the boat and the wind ceased. The disciples were "greatly amazed... beyond measure, and marveled. For they had not understood about the loaves, because their heart was hardened" (Mark 6:51-52).

The point of the whole story — the feeding of the five thousand, till the safe landing on the other side of the sea — is that when you fail to process truth your heart hardens. The result of a hard heart is that you will fail spiritually — you will fail others and you will fail God.

How do you know if someone has a hard heart? Look at how they dress, listen to the music they listen to, listen to their conversation. The focus of a person's conversation is a revelation of what is going on in their heart. The Bible teaches that out of the heart the mouth speaks. I am amazed how some people never talk about Jesus or the kingdom of God. All their conversation is about family, work, the weather, or play.

What is in your heart?

After the feeding the five thousand Jesus went immediately to pray. The disciples got in the boat to go to the other side of the sea. What you do after you encounter truth is critical. This is why so many believers are indifferent — they encounter truth and then they rush off to lunch, never taking the time to process what God has said.

Jesus Christ encountered truth and he immediately went alone to the mountain to pray, to process the truth. The disciples encountered the same truth and they got into a boat and faced opposition by the wind — a distraction. It completely took their mind off God and off of the truth encounter.

If you do not process truth immediately, you may miss the next encounter with God. It is written, "...and (Jesus) would have passed by them" (Mark 6:48).

You can be saved, be a Christian for years, come to church every week, and not get anything out of it but a social visit when you fail to process the truth. The result is a hard heart (see Mark 6:52).

How do you process truth? You don't let lunch, relatives or anything get in the way of your getting alone with God. Find a quiet spot and pray. Adjust your life to the truth, to the Word of God. Reflect on Christ. [24] Rebecca (Becky) Pippert Manley tells an unusual truth processing story in OUT OF THE SALT SHAKER.

In Becky's evangelism work on campuses across America, an agnostic student, Sue, once came to her. Sue's friend, Larry, had become a Christian. He had shared his faith with her and included her in many of his Christian gatherings. She respected the evidences of faith and love she saw in Larry and in the other Christians, but "I still don't believe," she told Becky.

They conversed for awhile, then Becky suggested that Sue "Tell God (or the four walls if that is the one you think you're speaking to) that you want to find out if Jesus is truly God. And that if you could feel more certain you would follow him. Then begin to read the Gospels, every day. Each day as you read, something will probably hit you and make sense. Whatever that is, do it as soon as you can."

Sue thought it was radical, but agreed. She began having what she called her 'pagan quite times.' The Christians around her prayed that God would speak to her through His word and give her concrete situations to obey Him in.

Several months later Sue came to Becky and shared, "One day I read in the Bible, 'If someone steals your coat, don't let him have only that, but offer your cloak as well.' For whatever reason, that verse hit me between the eyes. So I said to the four walls, 'Listen, walls — or God if you're there — I'm going to do what this verse says, if the opportunity arises today. I want to remind you that I'm trying to do things your way in order to find out if you exist and if Jesus really is who he says. Amen.'"

"The day went by and I forgot the verse. Then I headed to the library to continue working on my senior thesis. Just as I sat down at my designated thesis desk this guy comes up and starts yelling at me. He told me the school hadn't given him his thesis desk so he was going to take mine. (Everyone knows how important your thesis desk is for your work. The school only gives you one.) I started yelling back and pretty soon we caused quite a ruckus. But it was when he glared at me and said, 'Look. I'm stealing it from you whether you like it or not' that it suddenly hit me."

"I just looked at him and moaned, 'OHHHHH, no. No. I can't believe it.' And to myself I thought, 'Look God, if you're there, I do want to know if Jesus is God. But isn't there some other way of finding out besides obeying that verse? I mean, couldn't I tithe or get baptized or give up something else? But DON'T TAKE MY THESIS DESK!'"

"But I couldn't escape the fact that I had read that verse the very same day someone tried to rob me. Before, I had always been amused to see how Jesus aimed for the jugular vein in his conversations with people in the Bible. But now it didn't feel so funny. I took a deep breath, tried not to swear and said, 'OK, you can have the desk.'"

Just when the situation might have come to its end, the librarian approached them, outraged by what she had overheard from the boy. In a snowballing sequence of events, both he & Sue were led before four more levels of school officials before one of them finally turned to Sue and said, 'Well, what does Sue think we should do?'

"Even though I was not a Christian...I'd seen Jesus in the Bible. I felt drawn to Him. I realized, even without a thesis desk, somehow I still had more than this poor pathetic boy. I told them he could have the desk and the meeting was over. But when we walked out the door this guy grabbed my arm and asked me why in the world I let him have it. I told him he would think I'd really flipped out, but

I was trying to discover if Jesus was really who He claimed to be. I was attempting to do the things He told us to do. 'I've been reading what He says in the gospels. And today I read that if somebody tried to rip me off I was supposed to let them and even throw in something extra to boot.' All I could see were the whites of his eyes. 'So I'm going to give you the desk but don't press your luck about something extra.'"

"Then he asked, 'Why in the world would Jesus say such a crazy thing?'"

"I said, 'Hey, if there's one thing I've learned from reading about Jesus and meeting some real Christians, it's that Jesus would give you a whole lot more than a thesis desk if you'd let Him. I know Jesus would give it to you. So that thesis desk is yours.'"

"As I said those words," Sue told Becky, "I just simply *knew* it was all true. I kinda felt like God was saying, 'Well done. That's the way I want my children to behave.'" [25]

Reflect on Christ.

Adjust your life to His truth.

Then expect further encounters with God. As you process truth you prepare the way of the Lord. [26]

In Genesis eighteen we read of the Lord's appearance to Abraham at Mamre (one of the places he built an altar). The Lord told Abraham and Sarah "Your wife shall have a son" (Genesis 18:10). Sarah laughed within herself at the Word of God, at the truth. God confronted Abraham and asked, "Why did Sarah laugh?" And then said, "Is there anything to hard for the Lord?" (Genesis 18:13-14). "But Sarah denied it, saying 'I did not laugh,' for she was afraid. And He said, 'No, but you did laugh" (Genesis 18:15).

When confronted with truth Sarah responded as we often do — with denial — with an 'I can't believe it' attitude. But Sarah was caught and she was confronted by the Lord. She denied it out of fear, but again the Lord challenged and confronted her. He knew what she did within herself — she laughed. Sarah quickly realized the omniscience of God, and confronted with truth, she processed the truth.

> By faith Sarah herself also received strength to conceive seed, and she bore a child when she was past the age, because she judged Him faithful who had promised (Hebrews 11:11).

This same idea is carried over in the New Testament. Paul writes, "And I thank Christ Jesus our Lord who has enabled (strengthened) me, because he counted me faithful, putting me into ministry, although I was formally a blasphemer, a persecutor, and an insolent man, but I obtained mercy because I did it ignorantly in unbelief" (I Timothy 1:12-13). Here Paul expresses a similar experience to Sarah's. Paul really knew what he was, but God saw through that and strengthened him for service and ministry in spite of his weakness and unbelief.

Too many times we allow our feelings to dictate to our faith. If we do not feel a certain way, we believe our faith is weak or nonexistent. Our faith can be weak, feeble and doubting, but God sees beyond what we see or feel. Faith can still be present. And that is what God responds to, no matter how small.

> And by this we know that we are of the truth, and shall assure our hearts before Him. For if our heart condemns us, God is greater than our heart, and knows all things (I John 3:19-20).

After Jesus was crucified the disciples went back to the upper room. They went back to a place they had previously experienced God.

When God spoke to Sarah, she was by the terebinth trees at Mamre (see Genesis 18:1). This was the place Abraham had built an altar (see Genesis 13:18). These texts teach us the importance of returning to the place God has been previously encountered. It is there where we often find ourselves expecting to hear God speak again. Our returning does not manipulate God to meet our needs, but it is evidence that we are seeking Him. In doing so we position ourselves to hear from Him again. The Bible teaches us that we only need faith the size of a mustard seed, and that with such faith we can move mountains. The mustard seed is the smallest seed but when it is planted it grows and develops into a large bush — so large that birds can come and nest in it.

Sarah had faith. Even though it was small, she still had faith and God blessed her faith.

Brother Yun, known as THE HEAVENLY MAN exhorts us — "Do you realize that God wants all Christians to be pregnant with the Holy Spirit today? He wants to give you a vision for His kingdom that originates from heaven, not from yourself. He desires that all of His children would be over-shadowed by His presence in such a way that they are changed and give birth to something in their lives that brings many into His kingdom. The message I want to share is that you must be willing to become pregnant by the Holy Spirit. When a heavenly vision comes to dwell inside of your innermost being, the whole direction of your life will be changed." [27]

Chapter Seven

FACING UNFULFILLED DREAMS
BY FAITH

These all died in faith, not having received the promises,
but having seen them a far off were assured of them and
confessed that they were strangers and
pilgrims on the earth.
Hebrews 11:13

W e have all had disappointments in life. Many of us have been disappointed with God. We have had dreams and ambitions that just did not materialize. We have prayed and prayed and received no answer. We call out to God 'Why?' I have had people come to me — sincere, surrendered to the Lordship of Christ type people — and say, 'Pastor, why, why did God not heal, why did God not provide a job before the foreclosure, why was my loved one not saved?' These are legitimate prayers and questions.

How is a person to face unfulfilled dreams and disappointments by faith? As you come to this part of the book of Hebrews you will be helped to realize that you are not the first person who ever had disappointments and unfulfilled dreams. Maybe it will help you to know that some of the greatest men and women of faith that ever lived, faced disappointments and unfulfilled dreams. Yet they were still commended by God for living by faith.

What causes disappointments and unfulfilled dreams? We expect one thing and we get another. We expect our marriage to be healthy and our spouse to be supportive. We expect our children to grow up and love and want to serve Jesus. We expect our children to get qualified, to have ambition to work, and to get a good job. We expect to stay relatively healthy. We expect life to be fair.

As we know, life is not fair. The good guys don't always finish first. The marriage takes work and the kids grow up and are often more influenced by their peers than by their parents. Our bodies age. We get sick. Jobs are lost. We know about disappointments.

Faith is not measured by what we receive but by how we respond to what we do not receive. None of these heroes of the faith received what was promised. But they were still living by faith when they died and were commended by God for their faith.

As you study the lives of many Old Testament saints they all had specific personal promises given to them, and many waited an entire lifetime to receive them. Abraham did not receive his son until he was one hundred years old. Noah preached for one-hundred-and-twenty years, by building the ark, before the first rain drop came. Moses was never allowed to see the children of Israel enter the Promised Land.

When you face unfulfilled dreams and disappointments you must remember that God is in control. God was in full control the entire time these saints were waiting for His promise to be fulfilled. Never try to interpret unanswered prayer, unpleasant circumstances and unfulfilled dreams as a sign that God has somehow lost control. God is never caught by surprise. He is never distracted. He is never out of control. Whatever is happening in your life has been sifted through the permissive will of God.

> And we know that all things work together for good to those who love God, to those who are the called according to His purpose (Romans 8:28).

Another thing that motivated these men and women of faith is that God spoke to them personally. Does God still speak today? Yes. We must learn to recognize the voice of God. "My sheep hear My voice, and I know them, and they follow Me" (John 10:27).

Listen for God's voice — God is faithful. Seek Him with all your heart. Trust God's timing.

Much of our disappointment is because God does not respond when we want Him to. We want God to respond on our time table but God works from a different time table. We work off of chronos or calendar time. God works off of kairos or perfect time.

> For my thoughts are not your thoughts, nor are your ways My ways, says the Lord. For as the heavens are higher than the earth, so are My ways higher than your ways, and My thoughts than your thoughts (Isaiah 55:8-9).

There are eight Hebrew words in the Old Testament that convey the idea of waiting upon God in the context of prayer. "'Waiting on the Lord,' is not, in the strictest sense always synonymous with prayer to God, yet it is so patiently a part of the praying heart, and it so perfectly expresses the primary attitude of the man of devout life toward God, that it has come to be understood in terms of waiting upon God in prayer." [28]

The temptation is always to take matters into our own hands. *Wait upon the Lord.*

The temptation will be to doubt God and the promise. *Wait upon God.*

Several years ago during a revival meeting in Florida God woke me at five in the morning and spoke to my heart. God told me that in three years my ministry would transition. I wept, prayed, and thanked God. I woke my wife and told her what God had said — I told her exactly what He said, 'Your ministry will transition in three years.' I told her I didn't know what it meant but I knew God had spoken to me. I shared this with only a few close friends. In time, I noticed that the further away from the promise I got, the harder it was for me to believe it. Doubt and unbelief tempted me. But in three years my ministry transitioned.

I believe that is how it always works. The further we get from the promise, from the word, the harder it is to continue believing in the word of promise. Even John the Baptist had doubts about Jesus toward the end of his life while he was in prison. He sent others to ask Jesus if it was all true. We never get beyond the point of being tempted — tempted to doubt.

"So then faith comes by hearing and hearing by the word of God" (Romans 10:17). Build your faith in these crucial times. Stay focused on the promises. Don't become overly attached to temporal things. Jesus Christ said, "No one, having put his hand to the plow, and looking back, is fit for the kingdom of God" (Luke 9:62). Life is filled with disappointments. Keep living by faith.

When Nebuchadnezzar was getting ready to throw Shadrach, Meshach and Abed-Nego into the fiery furnace because of their faith walk with God, this is what they said —

> …Oh Nebuchadnezzar, we have no need to answer you in this matter. If that is the case our God whom we serve is able to deliver us from the burning fiery furnace, and He will deliver us from your hand, O king. But if not, let it be known to you, O king, that we do not serve your gods, nor will we worship the golden image which you have set up (Daniel 3:16-18).

When facing unfulfilled dreams you have to settle the '*but if nots*' of life. You have to come to terms with the fact that our God is able. He is able to do anything and meet any need. But if He chooses not to, it is never a question of His ability — rather it is all about His purpose and foresight.

How does one settle the '*but if not*'? First we must come to terms with the sovereignty of God. Our God is in control. The word 'sovereign' is both a noun and a verb. As a verb it means to rule and as a noun it means 'absolute ruler'. God is the absolute ruler of all. He has never been out of control. God is always working for His glory and our best. Our best is always defined by scripture as that which will conform us to Christ. Sometimes what will conform us to Christ is not easy, comfortable, or pleasant.

Second, we must understand the faithfulness of God. God's faithfulness means that because He is truth, everything He says and does is certain. God is faithful. Because of the faithfulness of God, he is also unchanging. We can trust Him. God will always do what is right and best every single time.

Thirdly, we need to understand the Omni attributes of God. God is omnipresent — He is everywhere present all the time. There is never a place where God is not. He is omniscient — He is all knowing. He knows everything past, present and future. He knows the real and the potential, and He knows them all at the same time. He knows the outcome before the start. He is omnipotent — He is all powerful. All power resides in Him. His power is infinite and unlimited. All of these attributes are expressed in the providence of God. I heard this definition of providence some time ago: "The providence of God is the preservation, care and government which God exercises over all things that He created, in order that they may accomplish the ends for which they were created." [29]

When facing unfulfilled dreams, knowing the attributes and the names of God is an incredible benefit to our understanding.

Chapter Eight

PARENTING
BY FAITH

By faith Isaac blessed Jacob and Esau concerning things to come. By faith Jacob, when he was dying, blessed each of the sons of Joseph, and worshipped, leaning on the top of his staff.
Hebrews 11: 20-21

Probably nothing causes more concern in men and women than the area of children and parenting. In Hebrews eleven we find biblical examples of parents who successfully taught their children to walk by faith. None of these parents were perfect but they were successful in planting the seed of faith in their children and blessing their children. Their children responded differently. Some brought their parents great joy and others great grief. Some served God and others lived for their flesh. Abraham, Isaac, Jacob and Joseph are each mentioned when it comes to parenting. The stress is on the fact that they "blessed" their children.

What does it mean to bless your child? First, understand it is not about how much money you can leave your child. Many a child has been handicapped by having finances he did not work for nor is able to appreciate. There is nothing wrong with leaving an inheritance as long as the child is capable of handling money and resources responsibly.

Responsibility is key. I have been amazed to watch parents, who love God and the church, leave resources to children who have no heart for God or for the kingdom. The resources that God has blessed these parents with are then spent on the world and on satisfying cravings of the flesh.

The word used is "blessed." To bless is from the Greek word "eulogeo" and it means to speak well of.[30] The Hebrew word for bless is "ba-rak" it means "to endue with power for success."[31]

Parenting by faith involves at least three things.

First, it means that the parent has an abiding relationship with Jesus Christ that is real, vital, and meaningful. Your children know you are a Christian by the way you live. They know you are a true Christian by your speech and by how you treat other people — especially people who wrong you. They will not know you are a Christian simply because you have a church preference and because you have a certain value system and are moral. They will know you are a Christian by your scripture based values.

Next, it means your priorities are consistent with Scripture. You make adjustments in your life, your time, and your money, to walk in obedience to God. The body of Christ has priority in your family. You teach your family to be a part and not to depart from the church. You have a personal quiet time daily, where you seek God in prayer and scripture. Your faith is active and even audible. I can still remember when I was an eight year old boy and I walked in the room one evening and my father was on his knees with his faced buried in the couch, praying. My life is still impacted by that sight.

Finally, it means releasing your child at the appropriate times so that they can become men and women of faith also. Releasing them, letting them go. The goal of Christian parents is to raise children to become responsible Christian adults. Often times we try to hang on by controlling our children through financial resources, because we think they are not ready to handle the responsibilities of life. We will not let them stand on their own. There comes a time that the child must leave the home and become an adult, ready or not. If we do not start parenting with this objective in mind when our children are young, we will produce co-dependent adult children. We will release our children, one way or the other. At some point they will leave to start their own family or we will pass away and not be there for them. So we must parent by faith and understand that letting them go is a part of life.

Our opening text talks about blessing our children — "By faith Isaac blessed Jacob and Esau." In Genesis forty-eight we find the story of Jacob blessing Joseph's sons, Ephraim and Manasseh. In the blessing Jacob recalls the mighty acts of God in his life. Though he was not perfect, he had memories of God to tell. This was a great event in Old Testament times, the bestowing of the blessing. With it children went forth and lived with confidence. Without the blessing, many were never confident in life. The blessing gave the children a tremendous sense of being highly valued by their parents. At a specific point in their lives they were given words of encouragement, love and assurance from their parents. Note that these were withheld when they were young — after they reached a point of maturity the blessing was then formally bestowed.

> And Joseph said to his father, 'They are my sons, whom God has given me in this place, and he said, 'Please bring them to me and I will bless them (Genesis 48:9).

The parental blessing today, is all about communication with your child, at every age. It includes four things. It begins with an unconditioned love. Jacob kisses and embraces his grandchildren. The number one thing your child needs is your love and affection. It is unconditional love. One of the words Jesus used in scripture for healing was 'thcrapeia.' It means a therapeutic touch. Affectionately touching a child is therapeutic. Everyone needs to feel love expressed by proper touches and hugs.

The parental blessing also includes providing a true sense of belonging.

> Now the eyes of Israel were dim with age, so that he could not see. Then Joseph brought them near him and he kissed them and embraced them (Genesis 48:10).

When Jacob drew the boys near to him, he openly expressed his acceptance of them; they were a part of him. Today parents need to be sensitive to opportunities to express acceptance their children. A child does not have to live up to all your dreams and expectations to know they belong. Having a sense of belonging is crucial for one's proper development. Ephraim and Manasseh, were grandchildren, not true sons. They grew up in Egypt. They did not share in the family activities and festivities as the other siblings because they did not live there. They were very much aware that they were not entitled to the blessing, but Jacob's action towards them allowed them to truly know that they belonged. Belonging and acceptance is a major element in the parental blessing.

The parental blessing is our attempt to give our children a sense of value. When Jacob took Ephraim and Manasseh in his old trembling arms and embraced them, do you think they realized how valued they were? Yes. [32]

Then again the parental blessing includes sharing your personal testimony.

> And he blessed Joseph, and said: 'God, before whom my fathers Abraham and Isaac walked, the God who has fed me all my life long to this day. The Angel who has redeemed me from all evil, bless the lads, let my name be named upon them, and the name of my fathers Abraham and Isaac; let them grow into a multitude in the midst of the earth (Genesis 48:15-16).

Jacob gives his testimony and through this blesses his grandsons, his children, his family. Your children need to hear from you how you came to faith in Jesus Christ. They need to hear of the faithfulness of God and His provision. "…The God who has fed me all my life long to this day" (Genesis 48:15). Your personal testimony of the reality of God working in your life impacts your children.

As Jacob prayed his blessing on Ephraim and Manasseh he began by recalling the movement and blessing of God in his family history. This was more than a history lesson — he was giving them a spiritual heritage. By recalling God's activity in your life and by showing your children the spiritual markers in your life, you instill in your children a spiritual heritage. Jacob wanted them to know God also — he wanted them to have a spiritual hunger for God. [33]

> Let my name be named upon them. And the names of my fathers Abraham and Isaac; and let them grow into a multitude in the midst of the earth (Genesis 48:16).

Then Jacob gave them hope.

> Then Israel said to Joseph, 'Behold I am dying, but God will be with you and bring you back to the land of your fathers (Genesis 48:21).

Joseph had not been to his homeland for many, many years. Jacob was assuring him that he would again return to the land of promise.

A spiritual heritage is the most powerful gift and blessing. The greatest thing I can leave this world is not a big church or a great ministry. The greatest gift I can leave this world is my children, MaKayla and Colby, who know God and know how to discern the voice of God and the will of God. By this future generations are ensured a living testimony of Jesus Christ and of the grace of God. I am responsible to communicate to my child by my words and my actions the truths of God and God's word, from their birth until my death.

> Train up a child in the way he should go and when he is old he will not depart from it (Proverbs 22:6).

Chapter Nine

MAKING RIGHT CHOICES
BY FAITH

*By faith Moses, when he became of age, refused to be
called the son of Pharaoh's daughter, choosing rather to
suffer affliction with the people of God
than to enjoy the passing pleasure of sin.*
Hebrews 11: 24 – 25

When you read about Moses, it is easy to overlook the fact that his parents were people of great faith (see Hebrews 11:23). They parented their child *by faith*. They understood that God gave them this baby and this understanding prompted them to make decisions by faith. They decided to disobey Pharaoh's command. At the same time they were making a right choice by faith.

Every day we are confronted and challenged to make choices. Some of these choices are of little consequence. It really is insignificant if I wear dark blue sox or if I wear black sox. Because of the insignificance of these minor choices we make choices all day based on our personal preferences. Personal preference is seen in one's style of dress, one's place of residence, and the company one keeps. But the Bible tells us what pleases God, which is faith. So we must become very sensitive to the choices we make and make sure we make right choices based on faith.

Just as Moses parents made the right choice to obey God and to save their son from certain death, we must understand that our choices have an impact on those around us. Faith never waits until tomorrow. Moses' parents responded immediately to the situation. They had nine months to pray and seek God's guidance and when they could no longer hide the baby Moses, I believe, in obedience to God they made an ark (see Exodus 2:3). The same thing Noah did for the salvation of his family, Moses' parents did for him. They daubed it with "slime and "pitch" to seal it and secure it. The Hebrew word for "pitch" is "ze-pet" meaning to liquefy[34] and the Hebrew word for "slime" is "hemar" meaning bitumen.[35] Bitumen is a material that burns easily and is found in nature as asphalt. When Noah sealed the ark with pitch, the Hebrew word used in scripture is "kapar". It means to cover, specifically with bitumen. To cover means to atone for. When Jesus Christ died on the cross, His death provided atonement, a covering for our sin so that we could be saved.

Just as Noah put a covering on the ark, Moses' parents placed a covering on his ark. I believe they were providing atonement by their faith and obedience to God. The choices we make affect our families, our friends, our co-workers, and even our casual acquaintances. We must learn to make right choices by faith.

Moses was raised in Pharaoh's palace, but by God's providence he was also raised with his own mother as his nurse. Moses had everything the world said was important when he came to be a man. He had the wealth of Egypt at his finger tips. He possessed anything he wanted; he was the grandson of Pharaoh. He was known through out the land and no pleasure would be with held from him. Moses had everything the world says is important. But Moses walked away from it all. Moses made right choices by faith.

What did Moses choose by faith? He chose the people of God over the people of the world. Moses aligned himself with the people of God. Today we have the same choice set before us — will we align ourselves with God's people, the church, or will we go the way of the world? Everyday we face the temptation to go the way of the world — go the way of popularity, go the way of pleasure, go the way of accumulation of things, and go the way of power. Everyday these temptations challenge us and we must choose by faith to go the way of God and His people.

In HEART MIND STRENGTH, S. Krishnan tells of four stages that can easily affect our thinking. They are assumption, abandonment, adaptation and assimilation. Together, they lead to compromise.

The stages work themselves out in us like this: Assumption —"some aspect of modern life or thought is entertained as significant or superior to what I already know and therefore assumed to be true. The second step is abandonment — something traditional, of course, has to be discarded, i.e., everything that does not fit in with my new assumption." Krishnan writes, "We are not simply changing tactics; we are rejecting truth." Then, in the third step, adaptation — "whatever remains of traditional belief is adapted to fit into the new assumptions."

The result? "The gospel has been assimilated to the shape of culture. We need to understand the culture and stop it from influencing us." [36]

Moses chose suffering and reproach. Why would anyone choose these things? When you choose to go with God, others choices automatically follow suit. You cannot go the way of the world and the way of the Father at the same time. "That I may know Him in the power of His resurrection" — we all want to experience the power of Christ in our lives but to do so we must finish the verse — "and the fellowship of His sufferings, being conformed to His death" (Philippians 3:10). When you choose Christ, suffering will find you. You do not have to go looking for it. When you live for Christ you will live contrary to this world and the world system — and suffering will find you.

Henry Blackaby tells us that "There must be some point in your life where you can say — not just doctrinally, but experientially —"I have been crucified with Christ" (Gal 2:20). Only the living Lord Himself can bring you to that place. The cross must be experienced to be understood. The deepest meaning of the cross and its transforming power can only be understood experientially. Don't ever equate knowing a doctrine with having experienced the reality of the truth."[37]

The word suffering in the Greek means hardship or pain. Reproach in the Greek means to be defamed, chided or reviled.[38] None of us sets out for this to happen but if we live to God's glory it is inevitable. People will react against us. People will react against us because we live by a different value system and we march to a different drummer. We will face ridicule and persecution. We will be accused of being intolerant. The key is found in the statement that Moses "endured as seeing Him who is invisible" (Hebrews 11:27b). Moses never took his eyes off of God. He endured forty years in Egypt, forty years in the desert, and forty years leading the people of God. Moses was persistent in his faith. Moses discovered who he was. He was born a slave and raised a prince, but he chose right. He was a child of God.

Many people face an identity crisis today — they don't know who they really are. So they live making choices out of their own selfish will. They miss the fact that God made them for a purpose — an eternal purpose. Once you understand who you are in Christ you can then accept responsibility for your life and for the choices of your life. There comes a time for all of us to realize that we cannot live off of someone else's spiritual commitment or faith. Moses, when he came of age, chose. He took responsibility. And Moses' life had an impact on those around him.

Making right choices by faith is the challenge that comes to everyone of us every day. You must first choose Christ. Then you prioritize your life around Christ, around the church, around the Word of God, around prayer, and around intentional faith and obedience to God.

Chapter Ten

FACING ADVERSITY
BY FAITH

*By faith the walls of Jericho fell down after they were
encircled seven days. Who through faith subdued kingdoms,
worked righteousness, obtained promises, stopped the
mouth of lions, quenched the violence of the sword, escaped
the edge of the sword, out of weakness were made strong,
became valiant in battle, turned to flight
the armies of the aliens.
Women received their dead raised to life again. Others were
tortured, not accepting deliverance, that they might obtain
a better resurrection. Still others had trial of mockings and
scourgings, yes, and of chains and imprisonment. They
were stoned, they were sawn in two, were
tempted, were slain with the sword. They wandered about
in sheepskins and goatskins, being destitute, afflicted and
tormented — of whom the world was not worthy.
They wandered in deserts and mountains, in dens and
caves of the earth. And all of these having received a good
testimony through faith, did not receive the promise.
Hebrews 11: 30, 33-39*

A number of years ago while planning a ministry trip to a third world country, I went to my doctor and received several immunization shots. These shots protect you from acquiring certain diseases and sickness. If only all of life were that simple. If all we had to do was take a shot or a pill and nothing bad or unpleasant could happen to us. Such is not the case. You don't have to live long to recognize that everyone faces adversity. We face opposition, difficulty, and unexpected crises in our lives. Being a Christian in no way keeps you immune from these things. In fact there are times when because of your faith in Christ you will face adversity. We saw that with Moses in the last chapter. Because of our faith we will face difficulties, we will be misunderstood, and we will be ridiculed.

Where does adversity come from? One place adversity can come from is the devil. The devil wants to stop us from getting to the place God wants us to be and from becoming the men and women of faith God intends us to be. When the disciples were following Jesus he told them to go across the lake to the other side. As soon as they started out a storm blew up and opposition arose, trying to keep them from reaching the place Jesus wanted them to be (see Matthew 14:22-33). Whenever we follow Jesus we can expect opposition. Opposition and adversity can come through people — they can come through situations and circumstances — they can even come through nature as we see in this story. The devil will use what ever he can to distract us and to prevent us from moving on in obedience and faith to Jesus Christ.

Not only does adversity come from the devil, but we also face adversity from the world. When I speak of the world I am referring to the world system — the world's philosophy.

> Because, although they knew God, they did not glorify Him as God, nor were thankful, but became futile in their thoughts, and their foolish hearts were darkened. Professing to be wise, they became fools and changed the glory of the incorruptible God in to an image made like corruptible man —and birds and four footed animals and creeping things. Therefore God gave them up to uncleanness, in the lust of their hearts... (Romans 1: 21-24).

Belief in God can be a very dangerous thing when not accompanied by faith.

Ray Pritchard says, "Belief in God when not accompanied by faith is the first step toward moral reprobation. By nature men suppress the truth (see Romans 1:18) and suppression of truth leads to ungodliness. Ungodliness leads to wickedness. That wickedness leads to every kind of evil and violence. Paul is expressing that moral perversion comes from a perversion of faith. It is a dangerous thing to believe in God when not accompanied by faith."[39] As the world moves into all sorts of wickedness, suppressing the truth of God, it tries to squeeze us into its mold. The world pressures us to be like them. When we refuse and live by faith we face opposition and adversity from the world we live in.

Many times we face adversity because we make poor decisions. We fail to follow Biblical principals with our finances. We fail to follow Biblical principals with our time and talents. We become distracted by the world and we suffer the consequences because we make poor choices. Many people leave the church, but when a crisis comes they run back. Yes, I am glad they have returned, but you can't live life merely using God and His Bride as an emergency vehicle.

There are times, I believe, when God allows or sends adversity into our lives. Why would a loving God do this? There are times God wants to take us deeper in our faith and it will not happen in a climate of ease and comfort. When the mother eagle is getting ready for the baby eaglets to leave the nest, the first thing she does is remove all the soft down and leafs from the nest, making it uncomfortable. Now instead of resting in comfort the eaglets are forced to stand on their wobbly legs so that sharp sticks will not poke them. This in turn builds their muscle. Next the mother eagle will force them out of the nest, pushing them if need be. They try to flap their wings as they tumble downward, screeching in fear. At just the right time the father eagle swoops under them, catches them, and carries them back to the nest. Again their muscles are developing and the next day they do it all over again until they come to the time that they fly — they soar. Even so, God allows adversity into our lives so that we develop spiritual muscle and one day soar as he would have us to. "But those who wait on the LORD shall renew their strength; they shall mount up with wings like eagles..." (Isaiah 40:31). There will be times that God will corral a person so that he or she cannot be exposed or be part of certain things, so as to protect that person. You may have tremendous athletic ability but the opportunities never come. Why? Could it be that the omniscient God knows that a life of athletic success would push you away from Him, instead of driving you to Him?

The issue of adversity and opposition is not 'will it come?' *It will.* The issue is how will you respond? What will your reaction be? It doesn't matter if the devil sends it or if the world sends it — if we create it or if God sends it. We must respond the same way, we must respond in faith.

In Hebrews eleven we are confronted with the "others" — men and women who were tortured, who were left destitute and homeless, who even faced excruciating pain and death all because of their faith in God. Part of the purpose of this section of scripture is to show us that real, genuine, authentic faith endures suffering and pain as well as enjoys success and promotions. Thank God for the "others." We see in this section of Hebrews that some, by faith, subdued kingdoms while others, by faith, were slain by the sword. Yet God says "they all were commended for their faith…" (Hebrews 11:39). Faith is not measured by your situation — faith is measured by your surrender to God. Those who suffered and died in Hebrews eleven, the "others," received the same commendation as those who subdued kingdoms. Faith is not measured by circumstances or situations but by your personal surrender to God. God is in control of all circumstances. You are to trust God in favorable and unfavorable situations.

When facing adversity you must have strong convictions about God. Real faith is living a life with confidence and conviction in who God is. In our conversations with other believers, the questions we must ask are 'What are your convictions about God? — about the Word of God?' We ought to invite conversation — 'Tell me about your knowledge of God, tell me about your times in His Word'. Our convictions about God and His Word must be so strong that we would gladly sacrifice any convenience or comfort for the sake of the kingdom of God.

A cartoon depicted two men deep in conversation — 'Do you think a man ought to be willing to die for his convictions?' asked the first. 'Certainly, that's why I'm careful not to develop any,' responded the second. [40]

"Of whom the world was not worthy..." (Hebrews 11:38). When you face adversity by faith, the very character of Christ flows from your life. "For whom He foreknew, He also predestined, to be conformed to the image of His Son..." (Romans 8:29). It's all about us becoming like Jesus.

"Others were tortured, not accepting deliverance, that they might obtain a better resurrection" (Hebrews 11:35). They could have been delivered — they could have experienced supernatural deliverance. Why would they refuse it? They lived by faith — they saw through the eyes of faith and they saw a better resurrection. They lived to glorify the Father.

What are you living for?

Billy Graham once sat in the office of the Harvard University president. He asked, 'What is the greatest problem your students face?' The president stared out the window for a moment, then replied, 'Emptiness.' The biggest problem is that we spend our whole lives looking for something worth living for instead of something worth dying for. [41]

Stephen was the first Christian martyr — he died while living by faith. He died while offering prayers and praise to Jesus Christ. He died preaching the gospel to the lost.

> But he being full of the Holy Spirit, gazed into heaven and saw the glory of God, and Jesus standing at the right hand of God. And said 'Look! I see the heavens opened and the Son of Man standing at the right hand of God.' ...And they stoned Stephen as he was calling on God and saying 'Lord

Jesus, receive my spirit'. Then he knelt down and cried out with a loud voice, 'Lord do not charge them with this sin.' And when he had said this, he fell asleep (Acts 7:55-56, 59-60).

Did Stephen receive a better resurrection? Absolutely. When Jesus Christ ascended into heaven after his death, burial, and resurrection we are told that "He was received up into heaven and sat down at the right hand of God" (Mark 16:19). As Stephen was dying, he caught a glimpse of the risen Lord. His gaze was fixed to heaven and he saw Jesus Christ standing — no longer seated, but standing to receive him home.

That is a better resurrection.

The "others" paid the ultimate price to pass the faith on to us. "God having provided something better for us, that they should not be made perfect apart from us" (Hebrews 11:40).

Chapter Eleven

FINISHING
BYFAITH

L et me share a last illustration with you of what it means to live by faith. In the book GET IN THE ARK, Steve Farrar tells the true story of fire jumper Wagner Dodge. Caught in the middle of a terrible mountain fire Wagner and his men had no way to escape. Their only choices were to stand and be fatally burned, to turn and be fatally burned, or to run and be fatally burned. "Dodge and his fifteen men were trapped. Their options were closed. They had about sixty seconds to live before the fire swept over them. Suddenly Dodge stopped. He took out a match, lit it, and threw it into the shoulder-high grass in front of him. His men, watching from behind, thought he had lost his mind. There was no time to light a backfire. But Dodge wasn't lighting a backfire. He was lighting a fire. In an instant, the grass was ablaze in a widening circle." [42]

There was no escape.

"As the ring of his new fire spread, it cleared a small area of all flammable substances. It was not much of a safety zone, but it would have to do. He jumped over the blazing ring, moved to its smoldering center, wrapped a wet cloth around his face, pressed himself close to the ground, and waited. As he had anticipated, the surging fire wall rounded both sides of his small circle, leapt over the top, but found nothing to ignite where he lay motionless. Within moments the front passed, racing up the ridge and leaving him unscathed in his tiny asylum. He stood, brushed off the ash, and found he was no worse for the wear. He had literally burned a hole in the raging fire." [43]

"Two of his men saw Dodge motion with his hand for him to join him. But they ran around his fire, found an old rock slide that was relatively free from vegetation, and burrowed into the rocks.

The thirteen other men saw what Dodge had done, and decided they would be better off making a run for it. None of them made it through.

Dodge survived the fire by going against human instinct. Faced with the threat of fire, he lit a fire and jumped into it. Because he was willing to step into the fire, his life was saved." [44]

Dodge knew that fire cannot burn without a fuel substance, with out combustible material. He burned all the combustible material, jumped over the flame and was safe on the inside. He had to act on the truth that he knew.

This is how we exercise faith. We act on the truth that we know. The Bible is God's Truth. It is not enough to know it in your mind. You must act on it. Many people today claim to have faith but what they are expressing is not Biblical faith. They have confidence in their families and friends or their financial resources. True Biblical faith always starts with the truth of the Bible and the person of Jesus Christ. Jesus Christ said, "I am the way, the truth, and the life. No man comes to the Father except through me" (John 14:60). With true Biblical faith we trust nothing but Christ and Christ alone for salvation. With true Biblical faith we continually adjust our lives to the truths of God's Word and the leadership of the Holy Spirit, which will always be in agreement with God's Word.

While it is true that "We are saved by faith, alone — saving faith is never alone." [45]

One of my life verses for many years has been "Trust in the Lord with all your heart and lean not on your own understanding. In all your ways acknowledge Him and He shall direct thy paths" (Proverbs 3:5-6). Only as God opened up Hebrews eleven to me, as I wrote this book, did I again gain more understanding. Not my own understanding, but understanding that is released by faith. That is why understanding is mentioned first in Hebrews eleven — "By faith we understand" (Hebrews 11:3). Without understanding by faith, we will continue to lean on our own human, fleshly under-standing. All human understanding is sight. We are to walk by faith not by sight.

In the Greek, another word for understanding is "hiemi". [46] It gives a word picture of two streams merging into one. What a beautiful example of our mind and will flowing together with God.

Everything about us is going to be determined by how we understand. Our perspective on events, our mindset about the future, and how we spend our time is all based on our understanding by faith. Joseph Stowell writes, "When troubles invade our comfort zones, two needs rise to the top: the need for understanding (to find answers to the probing and disturbing questions that crowd our minds and souls) and the need for healing. Of the two, understanding is key to managing problems in life effectively to its ultimate outcome. Without the understanding that produces the right answers, there is no sense of direction and no hope in which to feel secure." [47]

Understanding always starts with God. That is how to begin understanding by faith. If we try and get understanding from our situation and work our way back to God it will never work. We must start with God and work our way to our situation. Until we understand God's place in our lives and in the circumstances of our lives, we will not have understanding by faith.

All through life we experience things. Some make sense and other things make no sense. But when we walk by faith and we receive understanding from God, we keep pressing on toward the high calling of God in Jesus Christ (see Philippians 3:14).

When you know the Son of God by faith and you walk with God by faith, you do not live for this world — you live for the next. The testimony of the Father to the "others" is that 'this world is not worthy of them.'

My prayer for my life is that I too will not live for this world but for the next. That I will live by faith — that I will live with my gaze fixed on heaven.

In the light of the structure of the total universe; in the light of our calling to exhibit the existence and character of God between the ascension and the second coming; in the light of the terrible price of the cross, whereby all the present and future benefits of salvation were purchased on our

Mark D. Partin

> *behalf — in the light of all this, the real sin of the Christian
> is not to possess his possessions by faith.
> This is the real sin.*[48]
> FRANCIS SCHAEFFER

ENDNOTES

All scripture taken from New King James Version, Holy Bible; 1979 Thomas Nelson, Inc.

1. Vincent J. Donovan, Christianity Rediscovered; excerpted in The Lord of the Journey—a Reader in Christian Spirituality; 1986 Collins
2. Strong's Concordance with Hebrew, Chaldee and Greek Dictionaries — #5287; 1975 MacDonald Publishing House
3. Ibid — #3539
4. Ibid — #8045
5. Webster's New Dictionary of English Language; 2001 Popular Publishing
6. Henry Blackaby and Claude V. King, Experiencing God: Knowing & and Doing the Will of God, member's workbook; 1990 LifeWay Press
7. Laird Harris, Gleason L. Archer, Jr., Bruce K. Waltke, Theological Word Book of the Old Testament (twot) Volume 2 — #2287; 1980 Moody Press
8. Ibid — #2360
9. Mike Harland and Stan Moser, Seven Words of Worship, the key to a lifetime of   experiencing god; 2008 Lifeway Publishing
10. Ibid note # 6
11. Elisabeth Elliot, a Slow & Certain Light; 1973 Festival Books
12. Ibid note #2 — #3346

13. HOLMAN BIBLE DICTIONARY; 1991 Holman Bible Publishers
14. The Chernobyl Accident: What Happened; June 5, 2000 BBC news article
15. A.N. Martin, The Fear of God sermon series; Trinity Baptist Church, Montville, New Jersey
16. Matt Woodley, Costly, Messy, Beautiful Obedience sermon; www.preachingtoday.com/sermons/series/gospelingenesis/gospelingenesis5.html
17. Jerry Rankin, SPIRITUAL WARFARE, THE BATTLE FOR GOD'S GLORY; 2009 B&H Publishing
18. Attributed to Jerry Bridges; www.tentmaker.org/Quotes/discipleshipquotes.htm
19. Attributed to Robert Murray McCheyne, in SHE WAS ONLY 22 – The Life of Helen Ewan by James Alexander Stuart
20. Attributed to Elisabeth Elliot, www.oChristian.com; quotes – Elisabeth Elliot
21. Ibid
22. THE PULPIT COMMENTARY, Volume 1; 1961 Eerdmans Publishing, Grand Rapids
23. Ibid note #11
24. Richard Blackaby, Heart Cry Conference, South Africa; 2005 sermon
25. Rebecca Pippert Manley, OUT OF THE SALTSHAKER & Into the World; 1979 IVP
26. Ibid note # 24
27. Brother Yun, Paul Hattaway, LIVING WATER; 2008 Zondervan
28. James Thomas, THE PRAYING CHRIST; 1959 Eerdmans Publishing
29. INTERNATIONAL STANDARD BIBLE ENCYCLOPEDIA (ISBE); 1939 www.internationalstandardbible.com/P/providence
30. Ibid note #2 — #2121
31. Ibid note #7, vol.1 — #289
32. Dr. Rick E. Ferguson, Bestowing the Parental Blessing; 1995 sermon

33. Ibid
34. Ibid note #31— #1023
35. Ibid — #683
36. Os Guinness, NO GOD BUT GOD; used in HEART MIND STRENGTH – Loving God with All You've Got, Sunder Krishnan; 2003 Christian Publications, Inc
37. Henry Blackaby, EXPERIENCING THE CROSS; 2005 Multnomah Publishers, Inc
38. Ibid note #2 — #3679 — #3681
39. Ray Pritchard, The Forgotten Doctrine: The Wrath of God; 1997 sermon
40. Source unknown; 1980s published sketch
41. Patrick Morley, SERVANT; 2001 Spring issue quote, condensed
42. Michael Useem, THE LEADERSHIP MOMENT – Nine True stories of Triumph and Disaster and Their Lessons for Us All, 1998 New York: Random House; retold in GET IN THE ARK, Steve Farrar; 2000 Thomas Nelson Publishers
43. Michael Useem, THE LEADERSHIP MOMENT, 1998 New York: Times Business; quoted in GET IN THE ARK, Steve Farrar; 2000 Thomas Nelson Publishers
44. Ibid note #42
45. Attributed to R.C. Sproul by Joe Rhodes, The Glory Of God; 2001 sermon series
46. Ibid note #2 — #4920
47. Joseph Stowell, The Upside Of Down; 1991 Discovery House Publishers, Grand Rapids
48. Francis Schaeffer, True Spirituality; 1971 Tyndale House Publishers

LaVergne, TN USA
14 March 2011
220003LV00002B/5/P